Sing-Song-Roundabout

Christmas

Songs composed by
Brenda I. Piper

Play scripts by
Frank Cooke

Longman

Acknowledgements
With thanks to Sarah-Jane Bailey B.A. (Hons.) Dunelm

We are grateful to Ward Lock Educational for permission to use the melody and words of "Love to the manger".

LONGMAN GROUP LIMITED
*Longman House
Burnt Mill, Harlow, Essex CM20 2JE, England
and Associated Companies throughout the World*

© Longman Group Limited 1986
All rights reserved. No part of this publication may be reproduced, stored in a retrieval system, or transmitted in any form or by any means, electronic, mechanical, photocopying, recording or otherwise, without the prior permission of the copyright owner.

First published 1986

Typeset by Oxprint Ltd, Oxford in 16/17 pt. Plantin (Linotron)

Printed in Great Britain at the Bath Press, Avon

ISBN 0 582 18943 8

Contents

Introduction

Story 1 – Christmas is Coming
1 Winter days
2 Christmas preparations
3 Pillow case
4 Presents for Mum and Dad
5 Giving at Christmas
6 Let Christmas come soon!

Story 2 – Nativity Play
7 Gabriel visits Mary
8 Bethlehem
9 God gave us His Son
10 The shepherds
11 The wise men
12 Love to the manger

Story 3 – Christmas Rush
13 Christmas time
14 There's joy in giving
15 Christmas tree
16 Children of the world
17 Christmas party

Story 4 – Christmas Present
18 Christmas Eve
19 Toyland
20 The mystery of Santa
21 Christmas news
22 God's Christmas present

Additional Songs
23 Christmas spirit
24 Santa's magic cave

Introduction

The plays and songs within this book highlight different aspects of Christmas, seen through the eyes of children. With school concerts and entertainments particularly in mind, they have been written to be of use to all teachers who wish to have effective yet easily learnable material, which at the same time stimulates thought and teaches social, moral and spiritual values.

The play scripts are designed to offer flexibility so they can be either learnt and spoken by the acting cast members, or narrated by one person, as if reading a story. (This latter might require the narrator to add links within the dialogues, e.g. "and Mum said . . .".) Whichever is preferred, the intended pleasure and effect should not be lost.

To enable a greater number of children to take part, the songs are not intended to be sung by the acting cast but by an independent group or choir.

Although the songs have been written to accompany the scripts, they can also be enjoyed independently by children anywhere.

Christmas is a wonderful time of year – it helps us reflect the past, enjoy the present and have hope for the future. It is the deepest desire of the authors that this book will promote all these.

CHRISTMAS IS COMING

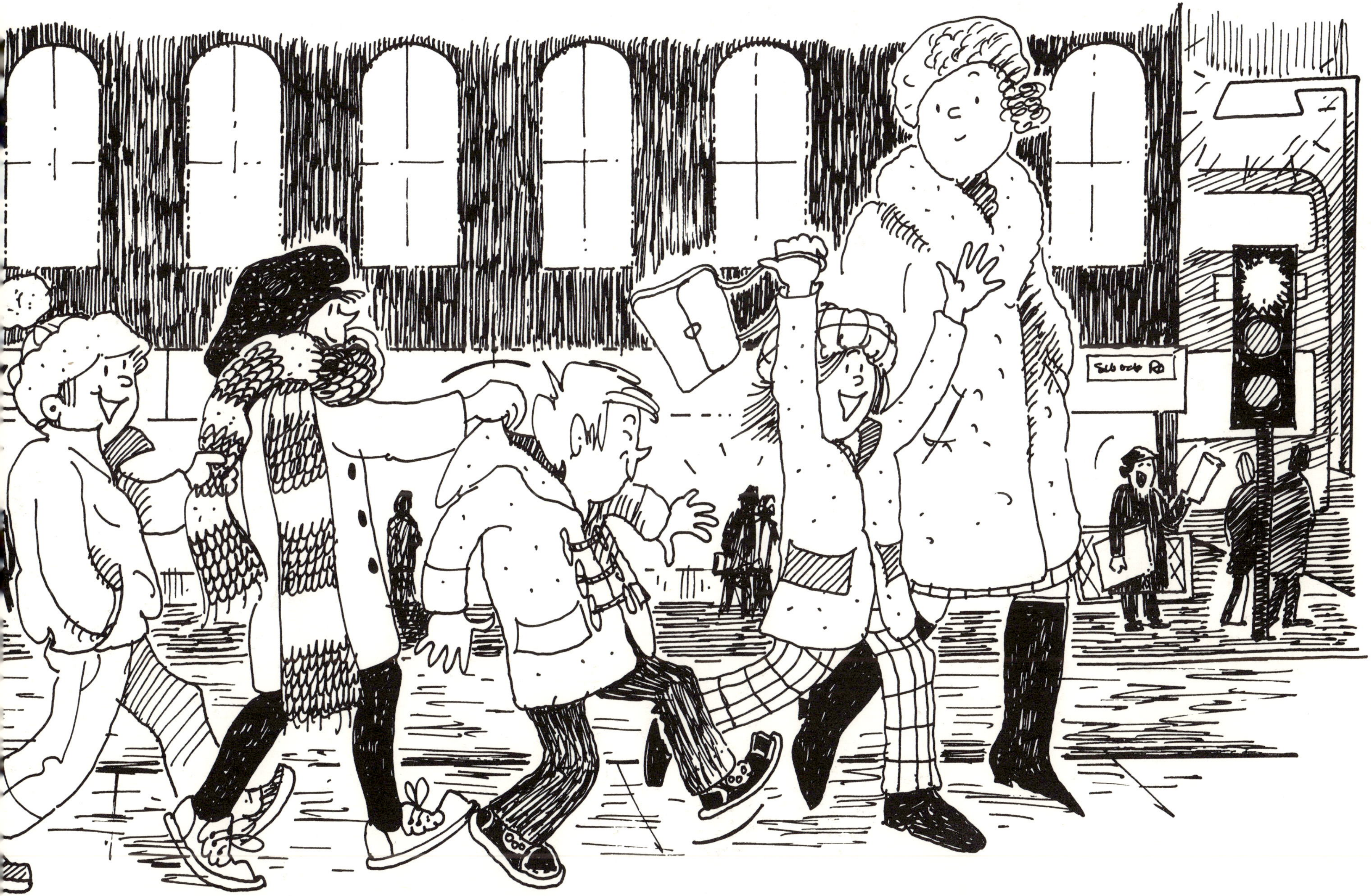

1 Winter days

NARRATOR It was the time of the year when the days were clearly getting shorter. It was already gloomy and growing dark as the children went home from school in the afternoon. The lights in the shops twinkled brightly against the darkening sky.

Jemma, who was a little older than her brother Jonathan, had been clearly instructed by Mum to make sure that Jonathan came home with her. She did this duty reluctantly.

One day when they reached home Jemma, who had not had a good day at school, said rather crossly, "I hate the dark days of winter" and catching her miserable mood Jonathan said, "Yes, and it will soon be really dark when we come home from school". And gloomily they said together, "I hate winter".

INTRODUCTION AND INTERLUDE

1. What is there to enjoy –
   During cold dark days?
   How we miss the bright blue skies,
   And warm gold sunshine rays;
   What can we look forward to?
   Is there something nice to do –
   During these long cold dark winter days?

2. What is there to enjoy –
   During cold dark days?
   How we miss the bright blue skies,
   And warm gold sunshine rays;
   What can help the time along?
   Is there happiness and song –
   During these long cold dark winter days?

2 Christmas preparations

NARRATOR: Mum had Jemma's and Jonathan's tea ready and seeing their miserable mood said, "Hey, you two – don't you know it will soon be Christmas?"

JEMMA AND JONATHAN: Christmas!

JONATHAN: When?

JEMMA: How long is there to go?

MUM: Not long, and after tea we can begin to get things ready for it.

JEMMA: It's simply ages away . . . weeks and weeks and weeks.

JONATHAN: Yes, it's weeks and weeks.

MUM: It will be here before you know it. Now, come on, let's make a start. I've got such a lot to do before Christmas. In fact, I'm going to make my list now.

With expression

INTRODUCTION AND INTERLUDE

CHORUS

There is such a lot to do ___ pre-par-ing for

CHORUS

There is such a lot to do –
Preparing for Christmas,
There is such a lot to do –
Preparing for that day.

1. There's the shopping for the food,
   Lots of presents and decorations;
   Christmas cards and of course new clothes –
   To wear for the celebrations.

2. There's the cooking of the cake,
   Christmas pudding and giant turkey;
   Sausage rolls and of course mince pies –
   To give to our friends and fam'ly.

3. There's the cleaning of the house,
   Grandma's staying and Grandad also;
   Ev'rywhere must of course be nice –
   Let's all try to make it be so.

3 Pillow case

NARRATOR "But what can *we* do to get ready for Christmas?" said Jemma and Mum replied, "Sit down now and write out a list of things *you* would like for Christmas. I am not promising that you will get half of them but there's no harm in asking!"

The children sat down and started to think. They knew from last year that they were not going to hang stockings up at the foot of their beds on Christmas Eve but pillow cases instead which hold a lot more. Here are some things they wrote.

1. Jem-ma knew what she want-ed to have

1. Jemma knew what she wanted to have –
In her pillow case,
Jemma knew what she wanted to have –
In her pillow case;
Some games for the video,
A dress and a radio;
That's what she wanted,
That's what she hoped for,
That's what she longed to have put –
In her pillow case!

2. Jonathan knew what he wanted to have –
In his pillow case,
Jonathan knew what he wanted to have –
In his pillow case;
Some trains with a lot of track,
A watch and an anorak;
That's what he wanted,
That's what he hoped for,
That's what he longed to have put –
In his pillow case!

4 Presents for Mum and Dad

NARRATOR	That's not all that was on the children's list, listen to this . . . .
JEMMA	a bag
JONATHAN	and a clock
JEMMA	and some chocolates in a box
JONATHAN	and some paints
JEMMA	and some games
JONATHAN	and some long white socks (*pointing to each other's list*)
JEMMA	and some books
JONATHAN	and some tapes
JEMMA	and some records to play
JONATHAN	and a bike (*gasp and pause*)
JEMMA	and a dog (*gasp and pause*)
JONATHAN	and an extra holiday . . . . (*the children then burst into giggles*)
MUM	You do want a lot. You'll need a magic pillow case. I only hope you're not too disappointed on Christmas Day. But now I want you to do something else. Write out a list of names and what *you* would like to *give* to each of them at Christmas.
JONATHAN	I would like to get something nice for Mum.
JEMMA	So would I and for Dad.
JONATHAN	Yes, and for Grandma and for Grandad.
JEMMA	And there's Sally, my best friend.
JONATHAN	There's Uncle Arthur too . . . Hey, how much money have you got saved up?
JEMMA	Only £7.23 and that won't buy a lot.
JONATHAN	I haven't even got that much!
JEMMA	Whatever can we get? Let's see what Mum says.

TIC-TOC

YELLOW PAINT

POP

INTRODUCTION AND INTERLUDE

With emphasis

1. What can a child buy for Mum — to make her Christmas bright?

What can a child buy for Mum — when there's nothing cheap in

1. What can a child buy for Mum —
To make her Christmas bright?
What can a child buy for Mum —
When there's nothing cheap in sight?

She'd love a new dress, some perfume and soap,
A necklace, a bracelet, some shoes and a coat;
If only children had more money to spend —
The gifts they would buy then would never end!

2. What can a child buy for Dad —
To make his Christmas bright?
What can a child buy for Dad —
When there's nothing cheap in sight?

He'd love a gold pen, a torch for his car,
Some cufflinks, a case, some ties and a scarf;
If only children had more money to spend —
The gifts they would buy then would never end!

5 Giving at Christmas

MUM It's not having a lot of money that matters. It's liking someone enough to want to give them a present – to show them you care. There is a sale of work at the Sports Club next week and there are bound to be some things on the Bring and Buy Stall which you can afford.

CHILDREN (*together*) Oh yes, let's see what they have at the Bring and Buy Stall.

CHORUS

Christmas is a time for love and caring,
Christmas is a time to give;
Christmas is a time for joy and sharing,
Christmas shows the way to live!

1. Think of mothers, fathers, sisters, brothers,
   Grandparents of our own;
   Uncles, aunties, cousins and friends –
   Who love to us have shown.

2. Give to mothers, fathers, sisters, brothers,
   Grandparents of our own;
   Uncles, aunties, cousins and friends –
   Who love to us have shown.

6 Let Christmas come soon!

NARRATOR Jemma and Jonathan went to bed happy that night but they were so excited that it took them a long time to go to sleep. They each had a tiny bedroom and kept calling to each other about Christmas.

With a swing — INTRODUCTION AND INTERLUDE

1. Let Christ-mas come soon ⎯⎯ it's the best time of the

1. Let Christmas come soon –
   It's the best time of the year,
   Let Christmas come soon –
   When Santa will call here;
   It always seems such a long way away,
   We seem to wait for it day after day;
   So, let Christmas come very soon –
   It's the best time of the year!

2. Let Christmas come soon –
   It is such a lot of fun,
   Let Christmas come soon –
   It's nice for ev'ryone;
   It always seems such a long way away,
   We seem to wait for it day after day;
   So let Christmas come very soon –
   It is such a lot of fun!

NATIVITY PLAY

Parts

Reader 1
Reader 2
Reader 3
Mary
Joseph
Herod
The Angel Gabriel
An Angel
Group of Angels
A Shepherd
Group of Shepherds
Three Wise Men

Christmas was now so near that Jemma and Jonathan and the other children had begun to decorate their school classrooms with paper chains which they had made themselves. They also put pretend snow on some of the windows. During the last week of term a Carol Service was held and parents were invited. A surprise item in the Service was a play. The teacher called it a Nativity Play and explained that it meant a play about the birth of Jesus. Jemma and Jonathan had been chosen to take part in the play. Although they had had many rehearsals, they were still nervous. But when the time came they enjoyed it very much, what with all the dressing up and all those people in the hall watching. It started like this . . . . . .

7 Gabriel visits Mary

READER 1	Nearly 2000 years ago a man called Joseph and a woman called Mary lived in Nazareth.
READER 2	Joseph was a carpenter.
READER 3	Mary was promised in marriage to Joseph.
READER 1	One day God sent the Angel Gabriel to Mary. She was afraid.
ANGEL GABRIEL	Do not be afraid. You have found favour with God. You will have a baby boy and you are to give him the name Jesus.
MARY	Let it happen to me as you have said.

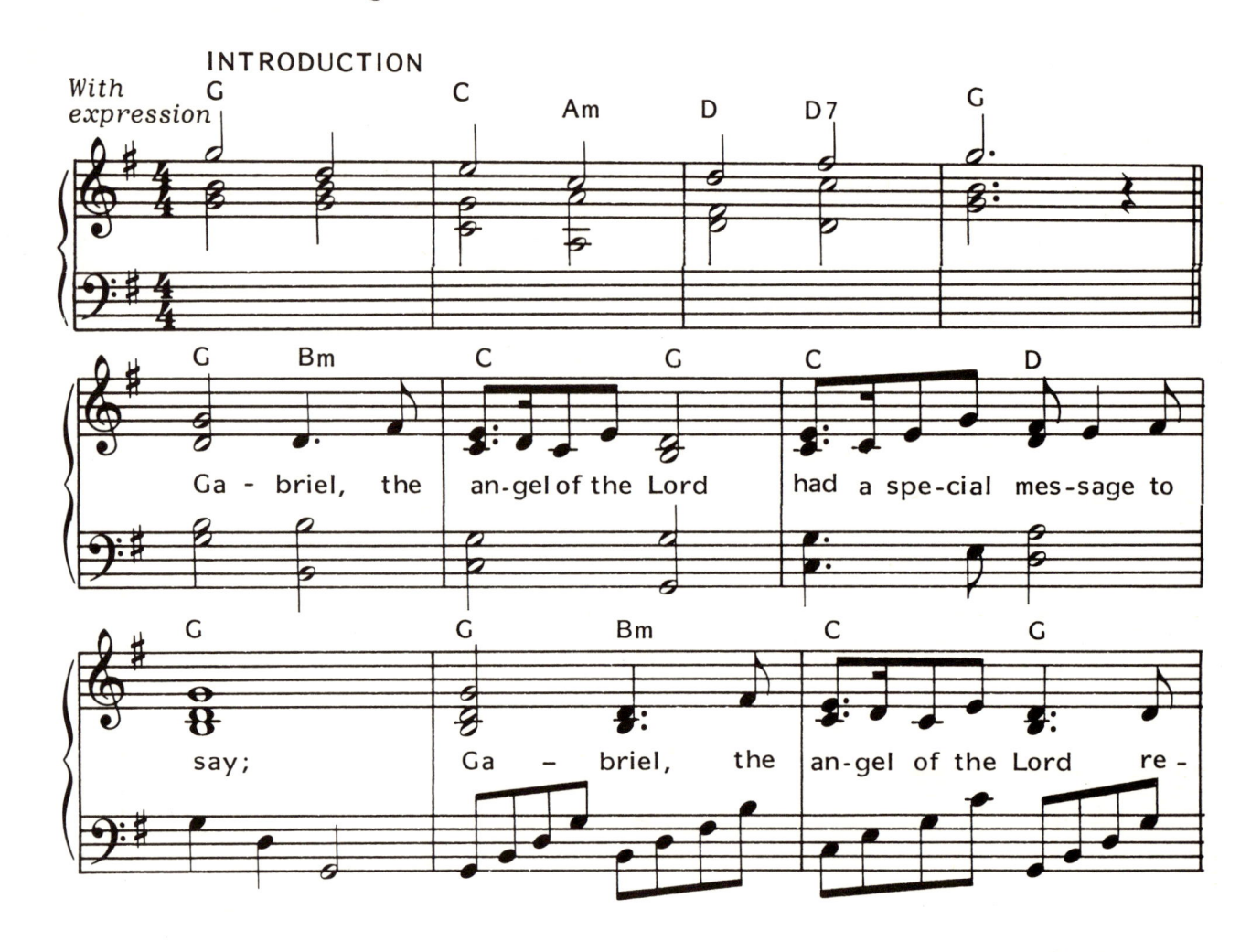

With expression

INTRODUCTION

Ga-briel, the an-gel of the Lord had a spe-cial mes-sage to say; Ga-briel, the an-gel of the Lord revealed it all to Mary one day. A very brilliant light shone right around, Mary fell down then to the ground; Gabriel's tender voice said, "Do not be afraid," Mary listened, then she

24

Gabriel, the angel of the Lord –
Had a special message to say;
Gabriel, the angel of the Lord –
Revealed it all to Mary one day.

A very brilliant light shone right around,
Mary fell down then to the ground;
Gabriel's tender voice said,
"Do not be afraid"
Mary listened, then she prayed –

I praise you Lord,
I praise you Lord,
I love you so with all my heart;
I praise you Lord,
I praise you Lord –
That in your plan I have a great part.

8 Bethlehem

INTRODUCTION AND INTERLUDE

Lightly

READER 1   Some time later the Emperor Augustus ordered a count to be taken of all the people in the Roman Empire.

READER 2   Joseph went from the town of Nazareth to the town of Bethlehem.

READER 3   He went to register with Mary who was expecting a baby.

1. The town of Bethlehem —
   Was full of people one night,
   And twinkling stars above —
   Shone their very special light;
   The Saviour of the world was going to be born —
   Before the sunrise of the morn.

2. The town of Bethlehem —
   Was full of God's love one night,
   And twinkling stars above —
   Shone their very special light;
   The Saviour of the world was going to be born —
   Before the sunrise of the morn.

9 God gave us His Son

INTRODUCTION AND INTERLUDE

READER 1 While Mary and Joseph were in Bethlehem the time came for the baby to be born. The inn was full so they had to take shelter in a stable.

READER 2 After the baby was born, Mary wrapped him up to keep warm and laid him in a manger. He was given the name Jesus, just as the Angel Gabriel had said.

1. God is good and full of love,
   God is good and full of love,
   God is good and full of love –
   Which He came to give to me.

2. God has giv'n His only Son,
   God has giv'n His only Son,
   God has giv'n His only Son,
   And He gave His Son for me.

3. Jesus is His precious name,
   Jesus is His precious name,
   Jesus is His precious name,
   And my friend He wants to be.

4. I should thank and welcome Him,
   I should thank and welcome Him,
   I should thank and welcome Him –
   In my life to stay with me.

10 The shepherds

READER 1 — There were some shepherds in that part of the country. They were spending the night in the fields taking care of their sheep.

READER 2 — An angel surrounded by a bright light appeared to them. They were afraid.

ANGEL — Don't be afraid. I am here with good news for you which will bring great joy to all the people. Your Saviour was born today in Bethlehem. You will find him in a stable and lying in a manger.

READER 3 — Suddenly a great many angels appeared from heaven singing praises to God.

ANGELS — Glory to God in the highest heaven and peace to all people of good will.

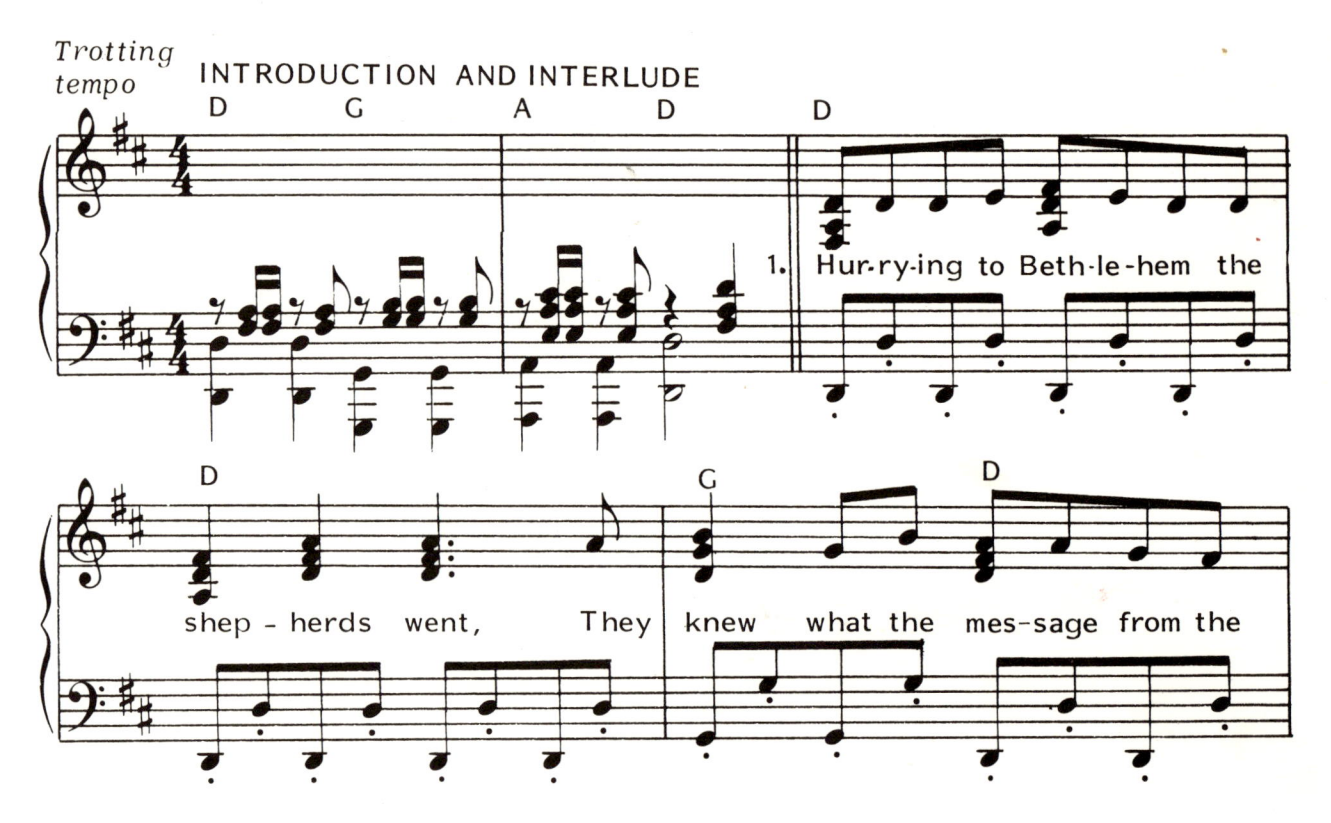

Trotting tempo

INTRODUCTION AND INTERLUDE

1. Hurrying to Bethlehem the shepherds went, They knew what the message from the

READER 2 — When the angels left them and went back into heaven one of the shepherds said:

SHEPHERD — Let's go to Bethlehem and see what has happened there which the angel has told us about.

READER 3 — So they hurried off and when they got to Bethlehem they found Mary and Joseph together with the baby who was lying in a manger.

1. Hurrying to Bethlehem the shepherds went,
   They knew what the message from the angels meant;
   They waved their crooks in the air,
   Felt God's presence with them there –
   On their way to Bethlehem.

2. Hurrying to Bethlehem the shepherds went,
   They knew what the message from the angels meant;
   They leapt up high in the air,
   Felt God's presence with them there –
   On their way to Bethlehem.

3. Hurrying to Bethlehem the shepherds went,
   They knew what the message from the angels meant;
   They clapped their hands in the air,
   Felt God's presence with them there –
   On their way to Bethlehem.

11 The wise men

READER 1 The shepherds went back to the fields singing praise to God for all they had seen and heard.

READER 2 Some time after Jesus had been born, some wise men who studied the stars came from lands far away. They had seen a special star. To them it was the sign that a new and very special king had been born. They asked where the new King of the Jews was to be found.

READER 3 At that time, Herod was King of the Jews and he was very upset that there might be someone who would take over his throne. He sent for the wise men and said to them:

HEROD Go and look for this baby and as soon as you find him, tell me so that I can go and worship him too.

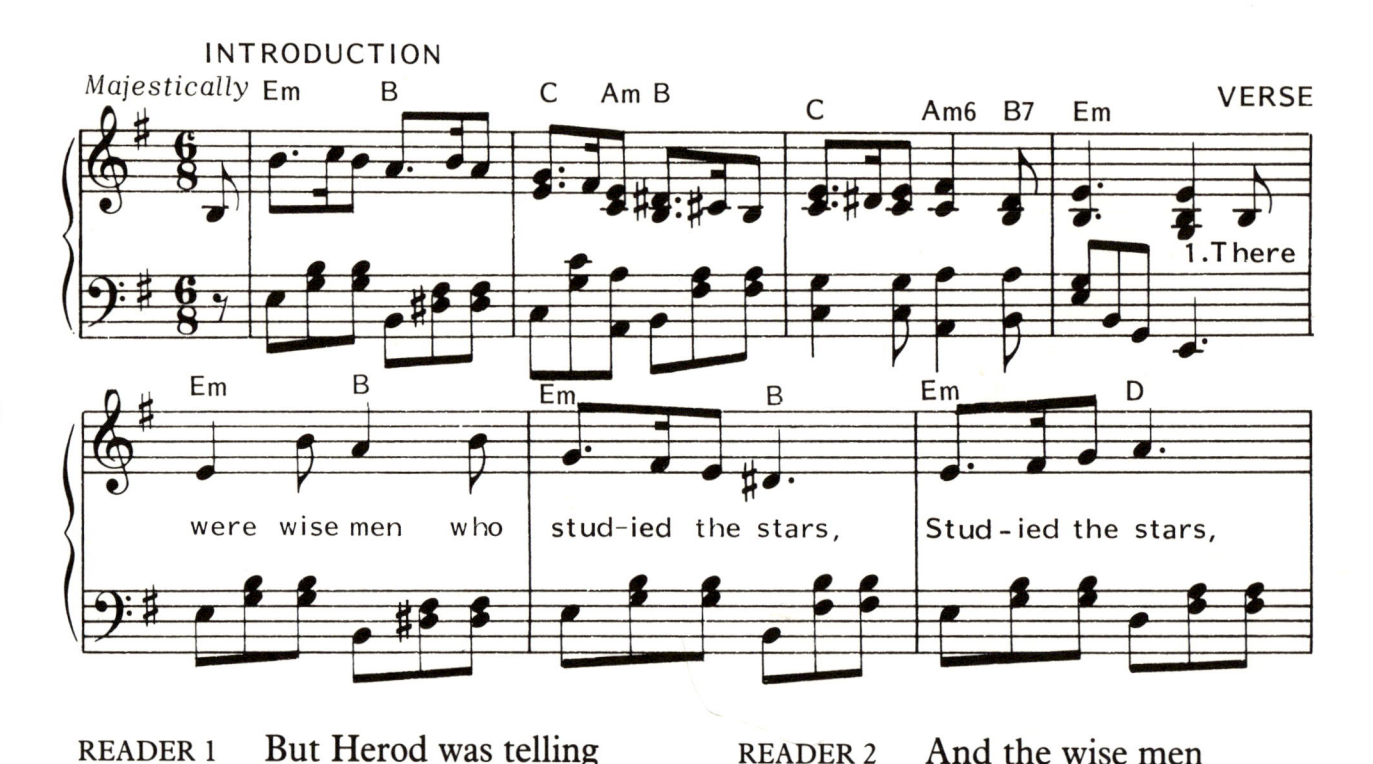

Majestically — INTRODUCTION — VERSE

1. There were wise men who stud-ied the stars, Stud-ied the stars,

READER 1 But Herod was telling lies. He wanted to kill anyone who might take his throne.

READER 2 And the wise men followed their star and it led them to Bethlehem.

1. There were wise men who studied the stars,
   Studied the stars, Studied the stars;
   There were wise men who studied the stars,
   Studied the stars.

2. One day they saw a bright eastern star,
   Bright eastern star, Bright eastern star;
   One day they saw a bright eastern star,
   Bright eastern star.

3. They travelled far and followed the star,
   Followed the star, Followed the star;
   They travelled far and followed the star,
   Followed the star.

4. They knew it meant a King had been born,
   King had been born, King had been born;
   They knew it meant a King had been born,
   King had been born.

5. They brought fine gifts and worshipped this King,
   Worshipped this King,
   Worshipped this King;
   They brought fine gifts and worshipped this King,
   Worshipped this King.

12 Love to the manger

READER 1 When the wise men arrived in Bethlehem, they went to the stable where Jesus was. They gave him the precious gifts they had brought with them. And then they knelt down, together with the shepherds, around the manger in which Jesus was lying.

So Jemma and Jonathan both played their parts in the school nativity play. It was brought to an end with many children dressed in different costumes from around the world. Each child brought a beautifully wrapped present to the manger. These were going to be sent the next day to poor children who would not have many things at Christmas. As they all went forward with their gifts, this is what they sang:

plus Away in a Manger.

INTRODUCTION
With expression and feeling

1. Many people came to Jesus,
   Many people came to Jesus,
   Many people came to Jesus,
   And gave Him all their love.

2. Shepherds left all their sheep to see Him,
   Shepherds left all their sheep to see Him,
   Shepherds left all their sheep to see Him,
   And gave Him all their love.

3. Wise men brought Him some lovely presents,
   Wise men brought Him some lovely presents,
   Wise men brought Him some lovely presents,
   And gave Him all their love.

4. Angels sang loud their joyful praises,
   Angels sang loud their joyful praises,
   Angels sang loud their joyful praises,
   And gave Him all their love.

5. They gathered all round His little manger,
   They gathered all round His little manger,
   They gathered all round His little manger,
   And gave Him all their love.

6. Let us together kneel before Him,
   Let us together kneel before Him,
   Let us together kneel before Him,
   And give Him all our love.

CHRISTMAS RUSH

SUPERMARKET

FOOD STORES

Happy Chr

Visit SANTA IN HIS Grotto →

13 Christmas time

NARRATOR Christmas was now so near that there seemed to be a kind of party spirit in the air. Christmas cards started coming through the letter-box at the oddest times. The decorated shops were packed with people. Coloured lights shone in the shopping centre. A huge Christmas tree stood in the middle of the town and tape-recorded carols were endlessly played through a loudspeaker. A man dressed up as Father Christmas was collecting money to buy things for people who had no-one to care for them at Christmas. Every programme on the TV talked about Christmas. You could feel the excitement as people shouted to each other, "Merry Christmas" as they hurried by.

Moderate tempo **INTRODUCTION**

You can feel it is Christ-mas, ___ You can

You can feel it is Christmas,
You can feel it in the air;
You can feel it is Christmas,
You can feel it ev'rywhere;
In the shops,
Along the street,
In the people whom you meet;
In the town,
In ev'ry sound –
You can feel it's Christmas time!

14 There's joy in giving

INTRODUCTION AND INTERLUDE

With emphasis

Chords: G G7 C Am G D7 G D7

CHORUS

Chords: G G7 C G G D

Lyrics: There's far more joy in giv-ing a-way, ___ Giv-ing a-way, ___

NARRATOR Jemma and Jonathan were so excited and without stopping for breath they chattered away about what they were hoping to get on Christmas Day. They whispered secretly about what they had bought for Mum and Dad and others. There were mysteriously shaped parcels on the top of Mum and Dad's wardrobe which they had been forbidden to touch. It was all so exciting. Seeing these parcels gave Jemma an idea and she said, "Let's wrap our presents up ready to give on Christmas Day". Jonathan agreed enthusiastically and asked their Mum to promise to stay in the kitchen until they were finished.

They started by putting on the table everything that they had hidden away which was now ready to be wrapped.

CHORUS

There's far more joy in giving away,
Giving away,
Giving away;
There's far more joy in giving away –
Than receiving on Christmas Day!

1. It's lots of fun to wrap presents up,
   A comb, a hankie or a cup;
   There's far more joy in giving away –
   Than receiving on Christmas Day!

2. It's lots of fun to see ev'ry shape –
   In Christmas paper, tissue or crepe;
   There's far more joy in giving away –
   Than receiving on Christmas Day!

3. It's lots of fun to hide gifts away –
   To give a nice surprise Christmas Day;
   There's far more joy in giving away –
   Than receiving on Christmas Day!

15 Christmas tree

MUM — You can put the presents you are giving under the Christmas tree.

CHILDREN (*together*) — Christmas tree? What Christmas tree? We haven't got one yet!

MUM — You wait 'til Dad gets home and you'll see what he is bringing with him tonight.

NARRATOR — Just then the door opened and Dad pushed through carrying a real, green, bushy Christmas tree which he began to set up in a heavy tub in a corner of the room, promising the children that before they went to bed they could help decorate it. They were so excited at this that they could hardly finish their tea fast enough. Soon they were all decorating the Christmas tree together.

INTRODUCTION

CHORUS *Strong beat*

Christmas tree, Christmas tree, O how I love you I will sing; Christmas tree, Christmas tree, Happiness you

VERSE *Lightly* [v. 4 & 5]

surely bring. 1. The lights all twinkle for all to see, The

N.B. For effect play verse an octave higher.

CHORUS

Christmas tree,
Christmas tree,
O how I love you I will sing;
Christmas tree,
Christmas tree,
Happiness you surely bring.

1. The lights all twinkle –
   For all to see,
   The lights all twinkle –
   For you and me;
   The lights all twinkle –
   So prettily,
   On the Christmas tree.

2. The tinsel glitters . . .

3. The glass balls sparkle . . .

4. The fairy doll poses . . .

5. The presents are hanging . . .

16 Children of the world

NARRATOR When they had finished, the tree looked beautiful and Jemma and Jonathan went to bed exhausted but very excited.
They were a long time going off to sleep but eventually they did and that night Jemma had a dream. In her dream all the boys and girls in her class at school were standing round a gigantic Christmas tree and instead of taking presents *off* the tree they were putting presents *on* the tree, and each present was labelled for children in different parts of the world. Four of the presents on the tree, however, were extra special and were for all children everywhere to share.

With emphasis — INTRODUCTION AND INTERLUDE

CHORUS

Children of the world wherever you may live, Precious things from us to you we want to give;

CHORUS

Children of the world –
Wherever you may live,
Precious things from us to you –
We want to give;
Children of the world –
Accept this gift we bring,
And hear these words for you we sing.

1. A parcel of peace,
   A parcel of peace,
   We give you ev'rywhere;
   A parcel of peace,
   A parcel of peace,
   We want you all to share.

2. A hamper of health,
   A hamper of health,
   We give you ev'rywhere;
   A hamper of health,
   A hamper of health,
   We want you all to share.

3. A deep jar of joy . . .

4. A locket of love . . .

17 Christmas party

NARRATOR When Jemma woke up she tried to tell Jonathan about her dream but he was not really interested as his thoughts were elsewhere and he said, "Come on! Get ready, today we're going to the Children's Christmas Party at the Sports Club". And sure enough, that afternoon they went to a Christmas party where they played games like 'pass the parcel', and noisy team games with balloons, and musical chairs.

With a swing

INTRODUCTION AND INTERLUDE

CHORUS

It's so nice to go to a par-ty, When Christ-mas Day is not far a-way; It's so nice to

CHORUS

It's so nice to go to a party,
When Christmas Day is not far away;
It's so nice to go to a party,
With lots of enjoyable games to play.

1. Pass the great big parcel,
   Pass the great big parcel,
   Join in the fun;
   Pass the great big parcel,
   Pass the great big parcel,
   Come on ev'ryone.

2. Sit down when the tune stops ...

3. Hide for 'hide and seek' now ...

4. Play the noisy b'lloon games ...

NARRATOR Once again, Jemma and Jonathan went home tired out and as it was so late they could not watch TV but went straight to bed thinking, "Isn't Christmas wonderful?"

47

CHRISTMAS PRESENT

49

18 Christmas Eve

INTRODUCTION AND INTERLUDE

Bright and spirited

CHORUS

Christ-mas Eve is here at last, It's mag-ic is so strong;

NARRATOR Dad had taken the day off work and early in the morning he called up the stairs to the children who were still in bed.

DAD Wakey-wakey, you two! It's Christmas Eve. We've exciting things to do today.

NARRATOR Jemma and Jonathan were soon out of bed. They washed, dressed and had breakfast quickly. They were looking forward to the day because everyone was in such a good mood.

CHORUS

Christmas Eve is here at last,
Its magic is so strong;
Christmas Eve is here at last,
Christmas Day now won't be long!

1 People are happy and full of cheer,
They're glad it's Christmas – that's very clear;
Christmas magic is in the air –
Ev'rywhere!

2 Bells are ringing and full of cheer . . .

3 Choirs are singing and full of cheer . . .

4 Children are tingling and full of cheer . . .

19 Toyland

NARRATOR Soon Jemma and Jonathan learned that Mum and Dad had a number of surprises in store for them. One was that they were all going out last-minute shopping and were going to have their lunch out. The children knew exactly what they wanted to eat and said:

JONATHAN Can we have hamburgers?

JEMMA And chips?

DAD Yes, let's all have a treat.

INTRODUCTION AND INTERLUDE

Brightly

CHORUS

It's a lot of fun when you go to Toy-land, Ma-ny love-ly things are there to see;

NARRATOR The children looked at each other. It's going to be a good day, they thought. Soon they were in town and found themselves in a big department store.

MUM I know you are quite grown-up, but would you like to go and see Father Christmas?

JONATHAN Oh yes please.

NARRATOR So they all went up to the toy department where the notice read 'NOW VISIT FATHER CHRISTMAS IN TOYLAND'. A lot of toys had been sold by this time, but both the children were wide-eyed when they saw the huge display. They pointed and chattered as they saw more and more lovely things.

CHORUS

It's a lot of fun when you go to Toyland,
Many lovely things are there to see;
It's a lot of fun when you go to Toyland,
Ev'ry child there will happy be!

1. Puzzles, board games, model kits too,
   Lots of dolls, computer toys
   – all brand new;
   It's a lot of fun when you go to Toyland,
   Watch out for the clown who waves
   his hand.

2. Soldiers, soft toys, story books too,
   Bicycles, cassettes to hear
   – all brand new;
   It's a lot of fun when you go to Toyland,
   Watch out for the clown who waves
   his hand.

3. Pictures, records, pedal cars too,
   Lots of games, houses for dolls
   – all brand new;
   It's a lot of fun when you go to Toyland,
   Watch out for the clown who waves
   his hand.

20 The mystery of Santa

NARRATOR Mum and Dad paid some money and Jonathan went into a dimly-lit cavern. He gazed at the models of Snow White and the Seven Dwarfs and reindeer. And suddenly . . . there was Father Christmas, sitting in a big chair and Jonathan was the next one to talk to him. Jonathan noticed his red fur-lined cloak, his wellington boots and all those whiskers which just looked like piles of cotton wool and with the red hood covering his head. Jonathan could hardly see his face at all. "What do you want for Christmas?" the voice boomed at Jonathan. Jonathan stared and thought, "That's stupid. I've already told him all that weeks ago, and in any case, it's a bit late now". So Jonathan didn't say a word, and soon it was another child's turn to talk to Father Christmas. Jonathan went back to his Mum and Dad and sister who said, "Well?" but he only said, "He's not the *real* Father Christmas".

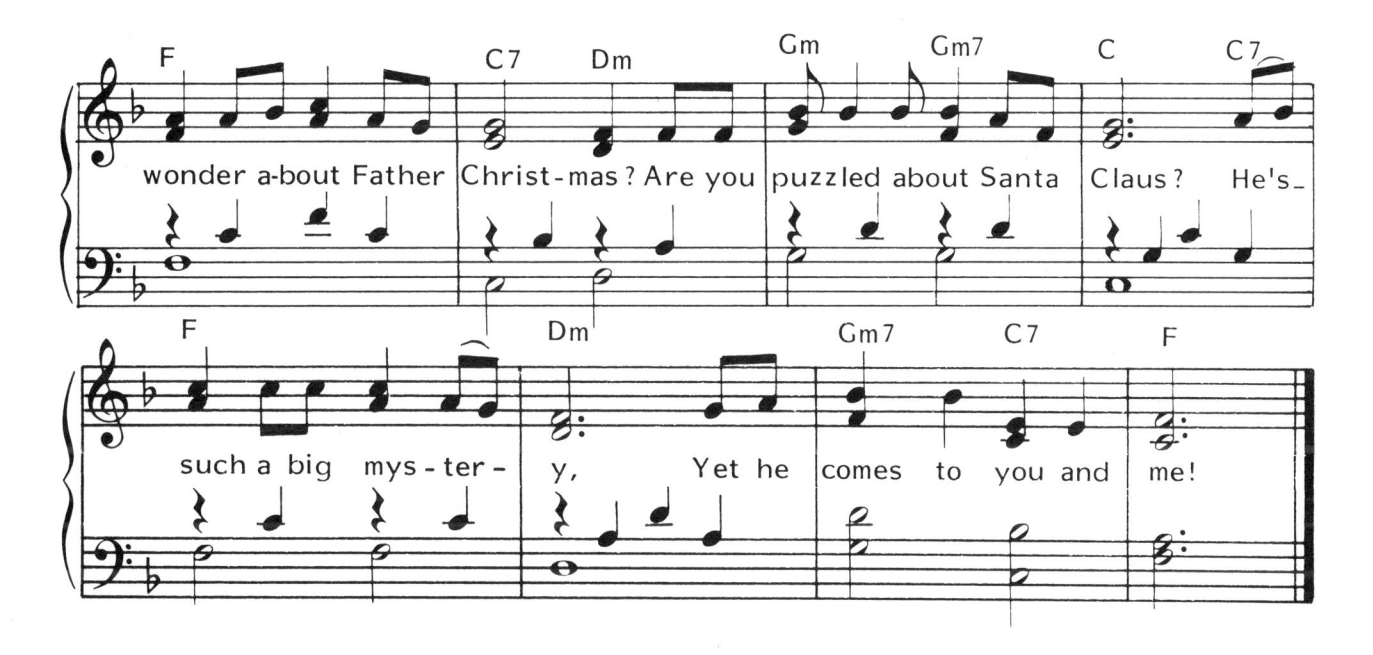

1. Do you wonder about Father Christmas?
   Are you puzzled about Santa Claus?
   He has always got so much to do,
   And his hours to get round are few;
   Do you wonder about Father Christmas?
   Are you puzzled about Santa Claus?
   He's such a big mystery,
   Yet he comes to you and me!

2. Do you wonder about Father Christmas?
   Are you puzzled about Santa Claus?
   He has never left soot on the floor,
   Or some snow by the bedroom door;
   Do you wonder about Father Christmas?
   Are you puzzled about Santa Claus?
   His reindeer can never be seen,
   Yet you know that he has been!

21 Christmas news

NARRATOR They all had a huge lunch at the hamburger place in the High Street and after doing some more shopping, they all went home. That evening when the children were watching TV, the door bell rang and before they could open it, they heard a lot of voices singing a carol at their front door. Mum said, "Turn off the TV and we'll all listen". Jemma and Jonathan, Mum and Dad stood in the hall and listened as the people sang.

CHORUS

Listen to the news,
Listen to the news,
Christmas time is here;
Listen to the news,
Listen to the news,
Sing it loud and clear.

1. Mary heard an angel say:
   "You are blessed so much today;
   You will have a baby boy –
   Who'll bring love and peace and joy".

2. Joseph had a dream which said:
   "You and Mary must be wed;
   She will have a baby boy –
   Who'll bring love and peace and joy".

3. Shepherds heard some angels say:
   "Christ the Lord is born today;
   Go to Bethlehem and see –
   The Saviour of the world to be".

4. God said: "Wise men from afar;
   Follow this my guiding star;
   You will see a baby King –
   And hear bells in Heaven ring".

5. Christmas is good news for sure,
   May we understand it more;
   Knowing why it all took place –
   For us through God's love and grace.

22 God's Christmas present

NARRATOR When they had finished singing, Dad opened the door and the choir shouted:

CHOIR Merry Christmas everybody.

FAMILY Merry Christmas to you.

MUM Come in and have some coffee and mince pies.

NARRATOR All the crowd trooped in and the children helped pass the mugs of coffee, mince pies and biscuits. The house was crowded and very noisy but no-one seemed to mind in the least.

When it was time for the choir to move on, Dad said, "Before you go, please sing something else".

And this is what they sang:

1 We thank you God now for giving
 your Son,
 for giving your Son,
 for giving your Son;
 We thank you God now for giving
 your Son,
 To show your great love on earth for
 ev'ryone.

2 We thank you God that He lived for
 us all,
 He lived for us all,
 He lived for us all;
 We thank you God that He lived for
 us all,
 And welcomes us to Him when His name
 we call.

3 This Christmas-time let us praise Jesus'
 name,
 let's praise Jesus' name,
 let's praise Jesus' name;
 This Christmas-time let us praise Jesus'
 name,
 For living and dying and rising again.

4 Some day to heaven He wants us to go,
 He wants us to go,
 He wants us to go;
 Some day to heaven He wants us to go,
 So always His wonderful love we can know.

NARRATOR Eventually it was bed-time for the children who were tingling with excitement. They hung up their pillow-cases and after saying prayers together, Dad said, "and no getting up at 4 o'clock to see if he's been!" But long after they had finished calling out to each other, Jemma and Jonathan lay wide awake wondering if they would even get to sleep. What if they stayed awake all night? Yet they did eventually drift off to sleep and it was as if they could still hear the choir singing as they lay there.

Additional Songs

The following songs are optional as they can be slotted into the stories if desired or otherwise sung independently during the festive season. They lend themselves to mime and actions.

23 Christmas spirit

With a swing — INTRODUCTION

1. Let your head shake –
   With the joyful Christmas spirit,
   Let your head shake –
   Come on ev'ryone and do it.

2. Let your arms swing . . . .

3. Let your hands clap . . . .

4. Let your hips sway . . . .

5. Let your knees bend . . . .

6. Let your feet tap . . . .

7. Let yourself rock . . . .

SUGGESTION

Follow the singing of each verse with the appropriate movement during the last eight bars of music.

24 Santa's magic cave

With expression

1. Father Christmas counted all his toys one day, And stored them safely all a-way; He hid them in his cave, And left them with a

wave; But some-thing mag-ic hap-pened that night ___ the i-cy cave was filled with rad-i-ant light, And the toys all spoke and be-gan to play in a ve-ry ex-tra-or-din-'ry way! 2. A fluf-fy dog pounced, And a big ball bounced; A ted-dy bear growled, And a cat mia-owed; A big top spun, All the toys had fun; And

1 Father Christmas counted all his toys one day,
   And stored them safely all away;
   He hid them in his cave,
   And left them with a wave;
   But something magic happened that night –
   The icy cave was filled with radiant light,
   And the toys all spoke and began to play –
   In a very extraordin'ry way!

2 A fluffy dog pounced,
   And a big ball bounced;
   A teddy bear growled,
   And a cat miaowed;
   A big top spun,
   All the toys had fun;
   And no-one ever knew!

3 Yes, a fluffy dog pounced,
   And a big ball bounced;
   A teddy bear growled,
   And a cat miaowed;
   A big top spun,
   All the toys had fun;
   And no-one ever knew!
   And no-one ever knew!

SUGGESTION

Dramatize as song describes and make the sounds mentioned at the appropriate time.